HOMAGE TO THE INCARNATION SUPREME

A HUMBLE DEVOTEE

Dedicated to the sacred memory of my Baba (Father) Late Debi Prosad Roy, Maa (Mother) Late Shubhra Roy and my revered Guru, Late Archana Puri Maa of Sree Satyananda Devayatan.

None of them are now on this earth in their physical forms. But, I have the strongest faith that they are always with me and guiding me at each and every moment of my life.

So, it is an honour to submit my offering at their lotus feet and seek their blessings.

Contents

Prologue

The Incarnation Supreme - Sri Thakur

Satyananda Dev

Homage to The Incarnation Supreme

Sri Thakur Satyananda Dev

Pearls of Divinity

Friends, it is my great privilege to place in your hands, my humble effort to offer homage to the Incarnation Supreme - Sri Thakur Satyananda Dev.

Sri Thakur Satyananda Dev (Sri Thakur to all His devotees) is the Human Reincarnation of the Supreme Godhead. And in sacred 'Guru Parampara' (Guru Tradition), He is my most revered 'Param Guru', i.e., Guru of one's Guru Dev. Though in human capacity, Sri Thakur (1902-1969) might have left his mortal coil before I was born, yet I strongly believe that the Godly Entity in Him is Eternal. That is why I have taken the liberty to pen this homage you are holding in your hands right now.

All our Scriptures have proclaimed "the companionship of the good" to be the ideal means of leading a life of virtue, the fountain-head of all joy and peace. And the study of the sacred lives of our God-Incarnates is the best path for cultivating such "the companionship of the good". This becomes all the more important during our current times, beset with so much uncertainty and so many challenges all around. Hence, the ever-lasting pole-star of God can be our safe anchor at this moment.

Hence this slim volume "Homage to the Incarnation Supreme" is being placed in your hands. Hope each one of you can find something of value for your own life here.

And the fragrance of Divinity of God-Incarnate always gets captured in His Holy Sayings. Therefore, it is my good fortune to place a sample of the sacred Sayings of Sri Thakur below. It is earnestly hoped that these **Pearls of Divinity** will bring a whiff of holiness into all our lives: -

- Holiness is the formula for this age. When you attain holiness, everything becomes possible.
- The essence of Faith in God lies in surrendering to Him.
- Go on performing your duty while constantly praying to God and repeating His Holy Name.
- The way is 'Faith' - Faith in the Grace of God.
- Keep moving forward by keeping Faith on one particular path.
- Keep on persevering towards your Goal with strong faith.
- To be virtuous, requires a strong will to be good, as its foundation.
- Ensure that you always keep repeating the Holy Name of God within your mind.
- Always keep your mind attuned towards the Higher Plane - be it in the spiritual matter or be it in the worldly affair.
- Always remember God is keeping watch over you - He is guiding you - keep this ever in mind.
- Through the habit of constant remembrance of God, we can create new channels of devotion to God in our brains. That is why Bhagavan Sri Krishna has laid so much stress upon 'Abhyas Yoga' in Gita.

- Just go on repeating the Holy Name of God - just go on praying to Him - He will make everything alright.
- Holiness is the formula for this age. When you attain Holiness, everything becomes possible.
- Be as pure as a flower.
- Holy Name of God is the only way in the present age.
- Whenever you pick up anything for study, then read it with wholehearted concentration - don't take up anything else - remember, a rolling stone gathers no moss.

With these words, I offer my homage to Sri Thakur.
With Pranam to Sri Thakur,
Debanjan Roy
Dated: 9th April 2022
(Sacred Chaitra 'Nava Ratri')

Foreword

A Personal Perspective

Friends, All of us are the children of our Divine Mother - She guides each of us in the right path all through our life - She takes care of us at every moment - She is always there for us.

However, beguiled by trifling temptations of this gross world, our own ego makes us think that life is meant for sole enjoyment during our good times - we don't even think of Maa then. The sensuous allurement of this transient life becomes all-in-all for us.

But, as all our scriptures have said, the wheels of this 'Sansar' (worldly life) keep on turning constantly. And so, one day, we inevitably find ourselves screaming under the burden of sorrows of life. And I personally believe the death of our parents is the single biggest among such tragedies. That mounting load of our anguish makes us get rudely jolted awake from our temporary spell of worldliness: we then start desperately yearning for the eternal refuge of Maa.

This is what that happened in my life too. Misguided by the false tinsel of this world, I kept on running after the acquisition of this degree, acquisition of that degree, striving for this job, striving for that job, hankering after that lucrative career, capitulating to pressures of getting married, and so on and so forth. It was a never-ending cycle of merry-go-round after the false material pleasures of this transient world. And this endless rat-race continued till I had a hard crash landing and then life seem like an ocean of sorrow.

It was in this background, besieged and tossed about by the waves of sorrows of the world, that I suddenly discovered the safe haven of Sri Satyananda Devayatan in the locality of Jadavpur in South Kolkata - the year was 2006. And I did not have even the slightest idea of who Sri Satyananda was at that point of time.

Still, the environ of that oasis was so soothing that, as they say, I got hooked with the very first visit and that spurred my interest in Spiritual life - a life about which I was completely ignorant till then. Subsequently, that one single visit made me go to this hallowed Institution of peace regularly, as I started slowly realizing how spirituality leads to a higher trajectory in life.

Here I was destined to meet my Guru Sri Archana Puri Maa and get blessed by her with the sacred 'Mantra Diksha' (spiritual initiation) in the same year. Then gradually, I came to know more and more about Sri Thakur Satyananda, the presiding Deity of our holy Ashram.

And slowly I started getting transformed by invisible Divine touch as I began reading the rich treasure of spiritual literature, listening to the mellifluous strains of Devotional music, taking part in prayers and cultural programmes, listening to the daily spiritual discourse of revered Swami Mrigananda ji (the revered President of Ashram) and so many other allied activities of Sri Satyananda Devayatan, that great sanctuary of serenity.

Thus, came about the inspiration in my mind to absorb a couple of drops from the infinite ocean of Divinity, Sri Thakur Satyananda and attempt offering homage to that endless expanse through a prayerful narrative.

Hope this account of reverence bless the life of everyone - let each one of us get sanctified through the

Divine 'Leela' of the Incarnation Supreme - Sri Thakur Satyananda.

So, with 'Pranam' to Maa, Divine Mother of the Whole Cosmos, here we begin... Jai Maa!

"The essence of Faith in God lies in surrendering to Him." - Sri Thakur

Preface

Objective of This Volume

Friends, as I said at the beginning of the 'Prologue', the prime objective of writing this volume is to offer my reverence at the lotus feet of Sri Thakur, the Human Reincarnation of the Supreme Godhead.

Just to let you know, the material of this book has been sourced from different authoritative texts on the sacred Life of Sri Thakur. And then, it has been complemented with my own perspective as His humble devotee. The primary basis of such a viewpoint has been my long association with Satyananda Order of Monkhood, which has enabled me to personally come in contact with respected Sanyasi and Sanyasini Mothers there. (Note: Sri Thakur was a stickler for addressing all ladies as mothers and His devotees follow the same tradition too.)

Since a long time, my primary pilgrimage centre has been Sri Satyananda Devayatan in Kolkata - the hallowed centre, where my late Guru, Revered Sri Archana Puri Maa used to be stationed at. In addition, I also had the privilege of sanctifying my life by visits to other holy ashrams of Satyananda Order at Baranagar (in Kolkata), Suri, Dubrajpur, Raasban, Batikaar (all in Birbhum district of West Bengal) and Dumka in Jharkhand.

In this manner, direct inspiration has been received through noble companionship of the respected Sanyasis and Sanyasini mothers. And indirect sources of my enrichment have been, first and foremost, deep study of the Divine literature of Sri Satyananda Order and then, various other means such as listening to the uplifting music of Ashram, interacting with different devotees, participating in various programs of Ashram, helping Ashram in various activities and so on.

Such inspiration has been moulding my spiritual consciousness continuously - this has led to my long-felt urge to offer tribute at the sacred feet of Sri Thakur through the medium of words. In this context, I offer my Pranam to the revered Swami Mrigananda ji, who always encouraged me in this direction.

However, due to heart-breaking upheavals in my own personal life, which included the most tragic death of my mother in 2015 (a tragedy with which I am yet to be reconciled) as well as loss of livelihood through loss of my job in 2016, this write-up of tribute to Sri Thakur - though planned and started in a preliminary manner way back in 2013 - could not be completed till date. For this gross negligence, for which I am alone responsible, I seek the forgiveness of Sri Thakur.

But Sri Thakur is ever graceful: through His blessing, I could resume this sacred task in the right earnest since January 2022 and complete it in the next three months. And while writing, I came to the inevitable conclusion that the expanse of the Spiritual charisma of Sri Thakur is so vast that it is impossible to condense it into one single volume. Hence, I request the Grace of Sri Thakur to allow me to pen a series on His sacred life in the days to come. The present narrative may be considered as the first volume in this series, where I seek to depict just the bird's eye view of His exceptional life, complemented with His holy Sayings.

Subsequently, separate volumes are proposed on individual aspects of His ocean-like contributions to all arenas of human Life: Religion, Spirituality, Humanitarian Service, Literature, Art, Culture, Man-making Education, Economic Livelihood, Compassionate Grace...the list is virtually endless!

So, I would like to submit all the above plans at the lotus feet of Sri Thakur and beg His Grace to enable me to complete this massive task. It will be like offering homage to Mother Ganga through her own waters!

And I thank everyone who has chosen to accompany me on this Divine journey.

"Holy Name of God is the only way in the present age."
- Sri Thakur

Acknowledgements

Gratitude is placed on record to the authoritative texts on the sacred life of Sri Thakur Satyananda. These authentic volumes have been penned by respected Sanyasi and Sanyasini Mothers of Satyananda Order in the language of Bengali. These are:

1. “Sonar Smriti” (“Golden Memories”), memoirs of Sanyasini Archana Maa

1. “Smritir Tirthe Satyananda” (“Satyananda in the Pilgrimage of Memories”), memoirs of Swami Nirvedananada ji

3. “Sharavana Mangalam” (“Listening to Divine Bliss”) compiled by Sanyasini Arati Maa

4. “Sobar Thakur Satyananda” (Satyananda, The God of Everyone), written by Sanyasini Archana Maa

“Shraddha is the main thing in life - it is Shraddha that propels a man forward in his life.”- Sri Thakur

CHAPTER ONE

Prayers

- God is our Divine Mother, Maa.
- Maa, we are Your children...please hold our hands, and lead us on the path of Righteousness at all times.
- Maa, kindly bless this humble effort to offer homage to Sri Thakur.
- Maa, with Your blessings, the Divine Journey Begins...

"Be as pure as a flower." - Sri Thakur

CHAPTER TWO

Leela of Avatar

Friends, as all our Scriptures and Sages have declared repeatedly, God Supreme is the sole entity in the entire Cosmos: everything in this Universe is nothing but an image of God. This is true for man as well – a human being is 'Divinity' personified at his core...his very essence is purity.

But alas! Man, at times, is found to indulge in sin also - this happens under the unholy provocation of 'sanskar', the impressions resulting from the accumulated action of all his previous lives. As a result, the Earth starts getting filled with the polluting vibrations of gross sensuousness. And when such moral degeneration crosses its limits, the Earth and its suffering humanity start desperately crying out for redemption.

Taking pity, God then descends in human form and gradually cleanses the earth of all its accumulated filth. **This is the Incarnation of Godhood.** In the holy 'Sanatan Dharma', such a Divinely merciful human form is called 'Avatar'. This blissful phenomenon has graced humanity multiple times in every single age.

Thus, Bhagavan Sri Rama Chandra, the Incarnation Supreme, descended in the 'Treta Yuga' and brought 'Dharma' back to this thirsty world. And thereafter, our

Earth was blessed by the Divine Aura of Bhagavan Sri Krishna in the 'Dwapar Yuga' and this world was again got rid of corruption, leading to the re-establishment of 'Dharma'.

This Divine tradition of periodic descent of Godliness continued, with the Incarnation of the Supreme Godhead in the 'Kali Yuga', with the births of Sri Buddha Dev, Sri Chaitanya Mahaprabhu, and then very recently, Bhagavan Ramakrishna Dev.

Sri Thakur Satyananda is the latest 'Avatar' in this Divine sequence to have blessed this Earth in our modern age. And given the wanton darkness of this age, he is the perfect 'Avatar' for bringing back Righteousness and restoring hope among His children.

In Srimad Bhagwat Gita, the holy Scripture of 'Sanatan Dharma', God has promised to Incarnate Himself again and again, to re-establish the might of 'Dharma' on this Earth and eliminate all the forces of 'Adharma' therefrom. Sri Thakur Satyananda's Divine incarnation took place under this noble promise.

With this short introduction to 'Avatar Leela' as the backdrop, let us now turn our attention to the sacred 'Leela' of Sri Thakur ... we begin by recapitulating the miraculous events surrounding His Divine birth.

"Self-knowledge, self-control and pin-point focus is the need of the hour." - Sri Thakur

CHAPTER THREE

Divine Birth

Friends, come, let us offer our homage to Sri Thakur through a peek into the wonderful account of his Divine birth...

In accordance with the Divine roots of 'Avatar', each and every attribute connected with His life - his birth, his growing up, his human appearance, his actions, his sayings, and so on - has an element of the extraordinary built into it!

And, as we look into the Divine birth of Sri Thakur, this assertion is found to be very much true. For this episode of Reincarnation, God chose Sri Mahendra Nath and Smt Kashishwari Devi, to be the fortunate parents. Now, for a long time, this Divine couple had remained childless - their first two issues had been stillborn - this had remained a continual source of anguish for them. The same agony tormented Kumud Kamini Devi (the pious mother of Mahendra Nath) too. Her long-cherished desire of a grandson had remained unfulfilled.

Hence, in desperation, she and her daughter-in-law decided to seek the assistance of Vilayet Ali (a well-known 'Fakir' - Muslim monk -belonging to Birbhum district in Bengal). The monk listened in sympathy to their sorrowful outpouring and assured them their longing for child-birth in family was going to be fulfilled at last. Then, he called aside Kashishwari Devi and instructed her as follows: "O mother! You'll have to carry out a difficult form of 'Sadhana' in a cremation ground. And if you succeed in satisfactorily performing it, you can rest assured of giving birth to several children in succession. Among them, your second child is destined to grow up into one of the Greatest Saints to have ever blessed this Earth." She immediately committed to Vilayet Ali that she would carry out all his instructions to the T.

Accordingly, both the ladies set out for cremation ground in the dark hours of night of an auspicious date indicated by Vilayet Ali. While Kumud Kamini Devi stopped at its periphery, her daughter-in-law fearlessly entered the solemn crematorium, sat down near a funeral pyre and performed the 'Sadhana', step by step, as per precise instruction of Vilayet Ali. At its conclusion, both the ladies came back home, brimming with full faith that the predictions of the monk would certainly turn out to be true. In due course of time, their faith was amply rewarded when Kashishwari Devi gave birth to a son, much to the joy of the entire household.

Two years after this happy event, she was blessed with a uniquely Divine experience - it was a holy precursor of the imminent descent of God in human form! It so happened that Kashishwari Devi was lying down one night at her home in Kolkata - her mother-in-law was also sleeping beside her. All of a sudden, she was startled to discover a wonderful ray of illumination falling upon her body, while the rest of the room was covered in the darkness of night. In that dimness, she could just perceive that it was coming out of the holy worship room, located in front of her own bedroom.

Puzzled by this unusual spectacle, she woke up Kumud Kamini Devi, who initially thought that, someone on the road outside must have been sending that ray of light inside their room from his torch. However, her visit to the worship room was enough to dispel that impression. There she witnessed the magical sight of a Divine ray of light emanating from the holy icon of Bhagavan Narayan! Now, Lord Narayan was the presiding Deity of household and His Image was enshrined on the sacred throne in worship room of the house. It was this light, travelling in the form of a ray, which was falling upon the supine form of her daughter-in-law.

On beholding this scene, she was filled with the deepest reverence - this Divine marvel gave her clear indication that Bhagavan Narayan Himself would be getting incarnated in human form in her own household soon! The prediction of the monk was about to come true - it was going to be the rarest of the rare blessings for the whole humanity - and thus, she felt truly blessed at that moment!

Many Divine happenings continued to sanctify her devout household. For example, one day Kumud Kamini Devi was a fortunate witness to the sacred sight of four Godly children, the eternal companions of Sri Gopal ji, dancing around her daughter-in-law!

Likewise, both Mahendra Nath and Kashishwari Devi were favoured with holy visions too. The former got blessed with the Divine spectacle of Sri Gopal ji sitting on the lap of Mother Goddess Durga! And the latter got cheered with the dream of a Godly child, handsome in appearance and wearing lovely anklets on his feet, roaming hither and thither in her room!

And the much-awaited day arrived at last! It was the season of Spring and as per lunar almanac, it was the month of Falgun. And this earth got glorified with the Divine appearance of 'Avatar' of Supreme Godhead, with the birth of the second son of Kashishwari Devi on the sacred 'Falgun - Krishna -Dwitiya tithi' (second day of the dark fortnight in the month of Falgun) at the City of Kolkata (then, Calcutta). As per the English calendar, it was the month of February 1902.

At birth, the infant looked as magnificent as the luminous rays of brilliant moonlight. However, to the worry of everyone, the baby did not start crying after his birth as expected - he continued to remain completely silent. So, the attending nurse frantically examined the new-born to make sure that he was alive. And it was a great relief to discover that everything was alright - only the eyes of the infant were shut tight - it appeared as if Lord Shiva Himself was deeply engrossed in the state of meditation!

In a further mysterious development, the lamp in the labour room went out soon after the birth of the Divine child. Surprisingly, the room still remained aglow with a soothing illumination - and at the same time, there began a mysterious shower of fragrant Lotus seeds all around Kashishwari Devi and her new-born son!

Soon, the whole room got filled with the sweet aroma of the Lotus flowers and to add to the wonder, the characteristic sound of wooden sandals softly moving atop the roof, could also be heard distinctly! All these magical signs gave clear proof of the special nature of the new-born infant! It also became clear that the monk Vilayat Ali had arrived in subtle form, to bless this Divine child!

And shortly thereafter, the new-born infant broke its worrisome silence and began to cry vigorously - on hearing that welcome sound, everyone in the household was overjoyed with relief!

It is well-known that miraculous incidents had preceded the Divine birth of each and every Incarnation of God Supreme. For example, all of us are familiar with the entire chain of charmed events that took place, just after the Divine birth of Bhagavan Sri Krishna in the prison of King Kamsa in Mathura. Similar magical events had preceded the birth of Bhagavan Buddha Dev also. And now, the same was true for the Divine birth of Bhagavan Saṭyananda Dev too!

On getting to know about such Divine happenings, a devotee always gets filled with a lingering sense of awe - for him, such events are direct evidence of the Grace of God in human life!

And now we shall turn our attention to the growing-up years of Sri Thakur...the Leela that happened during this period is equally wonderful as well!

“Go on performing your duty while constantly praying to God and repeating His Holy Name.” - Sri Thakur

CHAPTER FOUR

Glorious Years of Growing up

Friends, let us start getting to know more about the wonderful Leela that happened during the growing-up period of Sri Thakur. For the sake of convenience, we shall describe it in three phases:

i. Early Childhood:

With the passage of time, the Divinely blessed infant grew up into a child of lovable appearance. He was duly given the name of 'Satyabrata', which literally means the one, who always abides by truth - this was indeed the most appropriate description of an 'Avatar'.

And the loveliness of this child was comparable to that of a beautiful bloom of rose - everyone fell in love with him at the first sight! As a result, he soon became the apple of the eyes of not only everyone in his own family, but that of his neighbours as well.

By the time he turned three years old, Satyabrata had grown up into a child given to much mischief. So, he always had to be kept under constant watch. But given his naughty nature, Satyabrata's childhood soon came to be marked by many distinguishing incidents. One of them is related below:

One day, the mischievous child managed to give a slip to the alert eyes of his caretaker while playing outside. In a naughty mood, Satyabrata made a big jump from the elevated porch of his house onto the road below. But his playful antic resulted in injuries as his head got accidentally hit against a roadside manhole. However, despite being hurt, he remained absolutely unperturbed without uttering even a single cry - this was truly unusual for a small child of his tender age!

Later on, Kashishwari Devi a shock of her life, when she suddenly discovered congealed blood on the scalp of her dear son while feeding him on her lap. On subsequent interrogation of the caretaker, the worried mother came to know about the above incident - the wound of the child was at once washed, medicated and dressed up.

But in a sign of fascinating fortitude for such a small child, not even one drop of tear was shed by him, even while his wound was getting treated with astringent medicines! In the future too, such remarkable feats of endurance would continue to be displayed by Satyabrata, all through his growing up period. All these Divine portents gave a very clear indication: he was a born-Yogi!

The Divine essence of Satyabrata became evident in another arena: playfulness. While other children of similar age usually love to play ordinary games, Satyabrata's play was of a different nature altogether. One of his favourite games was to do the role-play of 'Dhyana'. In this unusual game, Satyabrata used to take up the role of a monk lost in 'Dhyana' while his younger brother used to play the role of his disciple. And during such times, his noble appearance, as he sat lost in 'Dhyana' with eyes closed, used to closely resemble the Divinity of Lord Shiva himself!

Often, as the Divine child used to start meditating, he used to get completely motionless. And in that absorbed state, he used to perceive his subtle inner essence escaping towards the infinitude of the sky, from within the shackles of his gross physical body. In fact, from high up in the sky, he could clearly see his own body sitting immobile in a state of 'Dhyana'.

And after the lapse of a finite duration of time, his subtle inner essence used to come back into his body. The unusual nature of such a meditative experience used to make him quite nervous - he used to worry if he was suffering from some mental aberration!

Much later, the Divine child - Satyabrata grew up into the foremost Saint of our times, Sri Thakur Satyananda and in the initial period of his 'Sadhana', he used to remain engrossed in the state of 'Dhyana' for 18 to 20 hours each day! And in that state, Sri Thakur used to get blessed with 'Samadhi'. Only then, he could finally understand that he used to experience the same state of 'Samadhi' in his childhood also.

i. Middle Childhood:

Satyabrata's character used to shine with numerous virtues right from childhood - indomitable courage was the foremost among them. A wonderful example can be cited here.

Once he was walking along the borders of a rice field, deeply absorbed in his own thoughts. All of a sudden, he was confronted with the frightening spectacle of a deadly cobra with its big hood up in the air, blocking his path. Any other child would have been terrified by the very sight of such menace. However, Satyabrata was absolutely fearless by nature - he just stood for a moment to consider his action in the face of that fearsome danger.

And thereafter, he performed an extraordinarily brave act: keeping his nerves steady, he simply jumped over the hooded snake and landed on the other side of the cobra! Then, he just sprinted away to safety. His bravery was witnessed and appreciated by all the farmers working nearby - they were simply astounded by the courage of a small child in the face of such peril!

Another novel quality of Satyabrata was his deep fascination with science and all its marvels. This Divine child had a passion for imagining scientific inventions, completely unheard of, in his time. For example, this gifted child had already solved the complexities of building submarine, torpedo, helicopter and so many other technological wonders! It was a sheer miracle that he could unravel the mysteries of such big inventions so early in his life!

And he was not content with just contemplating about those scientific inventions - he took great care to test their practicality as well! Towards this end, for example, this gifted child used to first build working models of a submarine and then, investigate their efficacy in the waters of the bathing tank of his own house!

All the incidents described above are just the tip of the iceberg of his childhood Leela...reams of pages will be required just to touch upon them!

iii. Schooling Years: -

Uprightness, love and kindness were the trademark virtues of Satyabrata. Under their noble influence, he used to make friends with boys of good character in his school (the renowned Hindu school of Kolkata) and constantly emphasize to them about the value of cultivating morality in all spheres of life.

His innate love and compassion became visible quite early during this period, as shown by the following chain of events:

Once Satyabrata came to know that one of his friends was sick. Immediately, he decided to go to that friend's house to enquire about his well-being. So, one day, setting aside his morning routine of going to school, he went to his friend's house instead. A few boys from his friend-circle accompanied him as well.

After reaching the house, Satyabrata conveyed his deep empathy and care by softly caressing the thin body of his friend. Neither any word could be exchanged due to the doctor's order nor was any word necessary as all communication took place from heart to heart. Thereafter, the boys sorrowfully came out and proceeded towards their school in a quiet manner.

On reaching their destination, they found that their classes had already started. And as Satyabrata reached his own class, he got rebuked by his teacher for his tardiness and was made to sit on the last bench of the classroom as punishment. Then the class resumed, but Satyabrata could not concentrate on what was being taught, as he was continuously thinking about his sick friend. The whole of his mind was overflowing with compassion for his friend.

All of a sudden, Satyabrata was put to a stern test, when his teacher could make out that he was not paying attention in the class - the annoyed teacher began to quiz him on what had been taught in the class since the very beginning. And to the amazement of his teacher and classmates alike, he could correctly answer each and every question!

The pleased teacher soon came to know about the benevolent reason behind Satyabrata's unusual delay in reaching school that day. At once, the remorseful teacher reversed his earlier punishment and allowed Satyabrata to come forward and resume his usual seat at the very front of the class. In this manner, the whole incident ended on a happy note and as they say, all is well that ends well!

It is aptly said that morning shows the day: the innate virtues of God- Incarnates always become apparent right from their childhood. This is true for each and every 'Avatar': Bhagavan Sri Ramachandra, Bhagavan Sri Krishna, Bhagavan Sri Buddha... And, as we saw, this is true for Bhagavan Satyananda Dev as well!

"The way is Faith: Faith in the Grace of God." - Sri Thakur

CHAPTER FIVE

The Transition to The Sacred Monkhood

All Incarnates carry the seed of Godliness within them since their birth - at the appropriate time, this seed sprouts and starts giving rise to a gigantic tree of Spirituality, that would give shade and comfort to the entire humanity one day. And as we'll see in this Chapter, this eternal principle was very much true for Sri Thakur also.

Satyabrata, in due course of time, finished his schooling and got enrolled in college to pursue higher education. Right from this point of time onward, he made up his mind to opt for the sacred path of 'Sanyas' and eschew the trifling pleasures of worldly life. The inner urge for this path, ever-present since his childhood, got transformed into a firm resolve at the starting point of his college.

So, on one hand, he regularly attended college; on the other hand, he continued his 'Sadhana' at the same pace at home. And now the sacred books of scriptures began to accompany him always: studying them frequently became his habit.

The noble path of spirituality thus came to co-exist with academics in his daily routine - during the day, he used to studiously attend his classes at college and on coming back home, he used to go back to his 'Sadhana'. Now, I shall relate a thrilling incident to illustrate the astounding level of his concentration during this 'Sadhana'!

One day, he was sitting in his room, completely absorbed in 'Dhyana'. And after a while, his younger sister happened to come in with a bowl of milk for him. However, she got the shock of her life to discover that, a huge cobra was already present in that room and the deadly serpent had spread its massive hood over her brother's head! The bowl slipped from her terrified hand and her frightened cries for help alerted the rest of the household, who rushed to Satyabrata's room! Fortunately, this frightening spectacle came to end after a while, as the cobra lowered its hood on its own and disappeared quietly.

The whole scenario represented nothing short of Divine symbolism: it clearly indicated to everyone that Satyabrata was Lord Shiva Himself - that's why the cobra, His ever-faithful companion had appeared, in order to pay its respect to the Lord Supreme! And, many such unusual events continued to occur, all of which pointed out to Satyabrata's Divine nature. In this manner, his Godly nature started gradually unfolding before his entire family!

In due course of time, Satyabrata completed his Intermediate, Bachelor's and Master's degree from the University of Calcutta. During this period, as his 'Sadhana' kept on increasing in intensity, it did not escape the attention of his alarmed family, who got worried that he would become a monk in the future and leave them forever. Therefore, his well-off family started trying their best to bring him back to the lures of the material world, through the temptation of marriage. Satyabrata, however, firmly refused despite facing repeated scolding from his father.

And at times, such family pressure used to get so intense, that once he even tried to end his life by trying to jump off the terrace of his house. Luckily, in the nick of time, his youngest brother managed to grab hold of him from the back and thus, save his life. Ultimately, Satyabrata's steadfast resolve to remain celibate, made his family capitulate. And thereafter, no further pressure was brought upon him for entering into marital bondage.

In this context, we recall how Bhagavan Buddha Dev grew up amidst the abundance of a kingdom and yet chose to renounce all such material riches in favour of the noble path of 'Sanyas'. The same trend was now visible in the life of Bhagavan Satyananda Dev also.

In this manner, each and every stage in the life of a God-Incarnate serves as a role model. That is why the study of their sacred lives is so valuable for us.

"The main thing is to surrender to God. He always protects the one who surrenders to him." - Sri Thakur

CHAPTER SIX

Magnificent Spiritual Awakening

Friends, from this chapter onwards, we enter into the Divine realm of the spiritual transformation of Satyabrata into Sri Thakur Satyananda. So, come, let us know more about this sacred metamorphosis process...

As Satyabrata's family gave up its efforts to get him married, he continued his 'Sadhana' with full fervour. Its intensity was truly remarkable! For example, in the heat of peak summer, he used to sit (without any cushion mat) on the searingly hot surface of the open terrace of his house at midday and in addition, wrap a warm quilt over his body for creating additional hotness! Then, in that blazing heat, he used to go on performing 'Japa' for hours together!

In a like manner, he used to sit for a long duration in the biting chill of winter on the bitterly cold surface of the same terrace and wrap-up himself in a wet cloth to escalate the degree of the freezing cold! And then, he used to go on performing 'Japa' for a long duration!

Many a time, he used to repeatedly hit himself hard on the back with a wooden dumbbell for increasing his own power of tolerance to pain! And, he used to go on practically starving himself day after day, by having just a small amount of boiled pulses in the morning and a little milk in the evening. And not even a drop of water used to pass his lips during the college hours!

Initially, as part of his 'Sadhana', Satyabrata used to meditate on formless 'Nirakar Brahma'. It was just like the 'Sadhana' of a 'Yogi' in 'Sanatan Dharma'. But one day, it so happened that while he was immersed in such 'Sadhana', a calendar picture of Divine Mother, 'Maa' came flying through the air and landed precisely on his lap. It happened all of a sudden. Now, this was a strange happening, to say the least, as no breeze of any kind was blowing inside the room, at that point in time!

As a startled Satyabrata quickly picked up the picture, he came to understand in a flash that, from then onwards he was being spiritually directed, to pursue the path of 'Sadhana' on the Divine Form of 'Maa'. Thereafter, Satyabrata decided to change the direction of his 'Sadhana'. He got that picture of 'Maa' framed and respectfully installed on the throne of sanctum sanctorum of his worship room. And then, he proceeded in the new direction of his spiritual practice with zeal. In due course, his 'Sadhana' got blessed through the Holy Vision of 'Maa'.

To further accelerate his 'Sadhana', Satyabrata decided to seek spiritual initiation from His Holiness Swami Abhedananda, one of the last surviving disciples of Bhagavan Ramakrishna Dev. So, one day he set out for 'Vedanta Math', the holy Ashram of Swami Abhedananda ji in Kolkata and on reaching there, he offered homage to his future Guru, who was taken by surprise to note the sharp contrast between his shabby outer appearance and his distinguished family background!

Afterward, as both talked together, Abhedananda ji could gauge the sincerity of Satyabrata's spiritual yearning.

And subsequently, on an auspicious day, he blessed Satyabrata with sacred 'Mantra Diksha'. Satyabrata's elder brother also had the good luck of being initiated by his holiness Abhedananda ji.

The spiritual zeal of Satyabrata kept increasing day by day. Sacred feelings of purity and renunciation constantly arose within his mind. In due course, everyone in his family began to revere him just like the holy image of God Himself. They were spellbound by the wonderful glow of spirituality that completely animated his entire being. Each of them came to gradually realize that Satyabrata had transcended the limited confines of his immediate family. Now he had become the source of Divine sustenance for the whole world. It was a truly remarkable happening!

After a while, Swami Abhedananda ji happened to establish his new Ashram (along with school and other facilities) in the scenic town of Darjeeling in north Bengal. He decided that Satyabrata would be the right choice as in-charge of this newly opened Ashram. But when he conveyed his decision to Satyabrata, he came to know that latter's family might not agree to release him.

Hence, Abhedananda ji came to Satyabrata's house to ask if his 'Shishya' would be released for the proposed assignment. Immediately his grandmother, father, mother etc. began to cry in unison and urged Swami Abhedananda ji not to take away Satyabrata, the apple of their eyes. However, they promised that he would be given unfettered liberty at home to pursue his chosen path of 'Tapasya'.

His Holiness Abhedananda ji, moved by such tremendous respect displayed by everyone in the family towards Satyabrata, blessed his 'Shishya' and directed him as follows, "Satyabrata, you will succeed in your 'Sadhana' in your home itself - you need not go anywhere else".

Satyabrata, who deeply admired his Guru ji, followed this instruction faithfully all through his life.

Thereafter, Satyabrata continued on his chosen path of 'Sadhana' with full dedication, while continuing to stay back at home, as advised by his Guru ji. And slowly, he came to look upon his family members as his own devotees! However, he removed all physical contact with them to the extent feasible and kept himself totally aloof within his own separate room in the house.

Here he used to remain completely absorbed in 'Dhyana' day-in and day-out and nobody could come except on absolute necessity. In addition, 'Puja room' on the second floor of the house was also kept specially reserved for him. In this manner, he kept preparing himself for 'Sanyas', the all-renouncing life of Monkhood.

Days passed and then came the most important day in the life of Satyabrata. For this occasion, he got a piece of garment, dyed in ochre colour - the sacred colour of 'Sanyas'. Wearing the garment, he went upstairs to the Puja room, shut its door and began his 'Sadhana' in the right earnest - throughout that night he kept performing the holy ritual of 'Homa', along with continuous prayers to Maa to bless his spiritual endeavours.

At an auspicious moment in the early hours of the morning, his prayer was granted: Maa Herself appeared before him and blessed him with the boon of 'Sanyas'. And Divine Mother also blessed him with a new name, 'Satyananda' - he thus gradually came to be known as Sri Thakur Satyananda among all his devotees, disciples and followers.

In earlier incarnations, Bhagavan Buddha Dev and Bhagavan Chaitanya Dev both had chosen to first renounce their family and then, adopt the path of 'Sanyas'. A new trail was now created by Bhagavan Satyananda Dev, who chose to stay back with his family in his own home and then, continue his 'Sadhana', which ultimately led to his getting blessed with 'Sanyas' by his Divine Mother.

And just as the first glimmer of dawn on the horizon results in a dazzling day afterwards, likewise the small spring of spirituality (that first came into public view with the opening of Sri Thakur's first Ashram at the town of Suri in 1939) gave rise to a vast ocean of Spiritual bliss in due course of time. In the next chapter, we shall be tasting a few drops of this ocean of Divine 'Amrit'.

"Just go on repeating Holy Name of God - just go on praying to Him - He will make everything alright." - Sri Thakur

CHAPTER SEVEN

Divine Splendour of Sri Thakur - A Glimpse

Friends, as stated in the very beginning of this book, Sri Thakur's Spiritual aura is so immense and multi-faceted that, we can only stand in awe in front of this vast ocean. So come, let us taste just a few drops of this nectar of Divinity and make our lives blessed...

7.1 Upholding 'Dharma', the Spinal Cord of India

7.1.1 Ashram

The lotus of the Spiritual genius of Sri Thakur began to bloom in a beautiful manner, as he continued his 'Sadhana' at his ancestral house at Suri, a town of Birbhum district in undivided Bengal. Slowly his silent 'Tapasya' began to attract the attention of spiritual seekers and they began coming in increasing numbers to seek his holy company. In due course of time, Sri Thakur established his first Ashram in that very house in 1939.

The unique feature of this Ashram was the fact that, besides adult devotees, many children used to come here every day, pulled-in by the Divine attraction of Sri Thakur. They used to love taking part in daily fun and games with Sri Thakur and the holy Ashram grounds used to, therefore, resound with the delightful sounds of laughter, clapping and merriment! And such fun and games became a channel of the flow of Spirituality from Sri Thakur to the tiny tots!

The daily activities of Ashram used to revolve around Puja, Japa, Dhyana, Arati, 'Mantra Diksha', Kirtan, Spiritual discourses, Cultural programs...it was a holistic picture of Spiritual life. The exemplary life of Sri Thakur himself was the biggest inspiration for everyone. Intense 'Tapasya' was the hallmark of his Divine life: a lion's share (18 to 20 hours!) of 24 hours in a day used to be earmarked by him for God while bodily necessities such as eating, sleeping etc. were relegated to the bare minimum! In a nutshell, his life on a day-to-day basis was truly Divine!

Over a period of time, Sri Thakur's spiritual fragrance spread with establishment of branch Ashrams at many places in Bengal such as Batikaar, Dubrajpur, Baranagar, Rampurhat, Kandi etc. and that in Bihar such as Madhupur, Dumka etc. All these Ashrams soon became the fulcrum of spiritual nourishment for large section of people.

"Strict discipline, integrity and hard work are what are needed." - Sri Thakur

7.1.2 Puja

Ashram life revolves around worship of God through 'Puja' - it is performed both on daily basis as well as on special occasions of the calendar. And in Bengal, the biggest of such occasions happens to be the sacred Durga Puja, where

Maa Durga is worshipped by her children over a period of five days in the autumn season.

Sri Mahendra Nath had earnestly wished that the holy ceremony of Durga Puja should be organized at Suri Ashram. On getting to know about his father's desire, Sri Thakur had prayed to Maa and received Her formal permission to organize 'Durga Puja' at Ashram. Four phases are visible in this celebration: -

First Phase: -

After receiving permission of Maa, the first Durga Puja was organized in September 1941. A beautiful ten-armed traditional image of Maa Durga was brought over from Kolkata and worshipped at the holy Ashram premises with the highest devotion. On such occasions, it was Maa Sarada, who was symbolically worshipped in the image of Maa Durga. The holy offering of flowers at the feet of Maa Durga used to be offered with a special mantra addressed to Maa Sarada. The annual ritual continued in this form till 1949.

Second Phase: -

From 1950 onwards, the next phase started with the completely new tradition of performing all the rituals of Puja in front of an actual image of Maa Sarada Herself. Initially, many devotees felt disheartened on the discontinuation of the traditional form of Sri Durga Puja. Then under Sri Thakur's Grace, they finally came to understand that Maa Durga was, in real essence, a manifestation of Maa Sarada herself. His inspiring words cheered up everyone and in due course, the Ashram grounds overflowed with large crowds, eager to witness such a unique form of Sri Durga Puja.

Third Phase: -

The image worshipped so far during Sri Durga Puja underwent a change in 1955. It had an interesting history behind it. The auspicious birth centenary of Maa Sarada came around in the year of 1954. To mark this memorable occasion, Sri Thakur began the tradition of organizing a large fair named ‘Sarada Mela’ in the town of Suri. An elegant image of Maa Sarada was specially crafted and then, installed in the main pavilion of that fair.

And from 1955 onwards, it was this image of Maa Sarada, which was worshipped during Sri Durga Puja at Ashram. Since this image was so graceful in appearance, Sri Thakur decided to keep it back at Ashram and not allow it to be immersed in water, as customarily done at the end of the celebration.

The fourth and the final phase: -

This phase commenced in 1958, when Sri Thakur received instructions from Maa that Sri Durga Puja should be started at Baranagar Ashram also. The idol of Maa Sarada was accordingly shifted from Suri to Baranagar. And in a unique practice, eight more hands were then added to this two-armed image, making it a ten-armed Image, holding one weapon in each hand. This wonderful ten-armed ‘Sarada-Durga’ Idol was then ceremonially worshipped over the customary five-day period.

Thus began the sacred tradition of Sri Sarada-Durga Puja at Baranagar Ashram, which continues till date, with the same purity of devotion, even after the passage of so many decades.

In like manner, the sacred Image of Maa Sarada is worshipped throughout the year as Sri Lakshmi, Sri Kali and so on. It is a really befitting way of respecting Maa Sarada in different manifestations of her own Divine self and stands as a unique contribution of Sri Thakur in the arena of Religion and Spirituality.

"Just go on repeating Holy Name of God at all times." - Sri Thakur

7.1.3 The beautiful Leela of Sri Gopal ji

In the Divine life of Sri Thakur, one of the loveliest chapters is the delightful Leela of Sri Gopal Ji. This was a tiny idol that had arrived in the household of Sri Mahendra Nath just a few days before the birth of Sri Thakur. Later on, that holy icon of Sri Gopal ji was brought over from the Kashipur household and ceremonially installed at Baranagar Ashram.

Thereafter, so many unbelievable instances of Divine Leela of Sri Gopal ji took place. Some of the instances are joyfully shared here.

Now, Gopal ji was very fond of watching the cultural programs, that were so tastefully arranged at Baranagar Ashram, round the year on different occasions. In this sequence, an all-night music program was being held at Baranagar once and Sri Gopal ji was happily listening to the songs of the artist on the dais, while cosily held in the lap of one of the Sanyasini mothers.

After a while, Gopal ji was lovingly put to sleep by his Sanyasini mother as he was literally looked upon as a living entity at the holy Ashram. And it is a well-known custom in India that, a small infant like Gopal ji is not supposed to remain awake the whole night. He is supposed to undergo refreshing sleep. But lo and behold! To the amazement of everyone, it was discovered that Gopal ji had sat up on his own, soon after he was put in his sleeping bed! Immediately, Sri Thakur gave the instruction that Gopal ji should be taken to the venue of the music program once again: He would like to enjoy the rest of the program as well!

In the same astonishing manner, Gopal ji would inevitably sit up during each and every journey by train or by car, while accompanying Sri Thakur. It used to straight away imply that, just like any other small kid, he also wanted to relish the passing sceneries of Mother Nature. So, his Sanyasini mother would oblige and hold Gopal ji in her lap, as He happily soaked-in the natural sceneries from the train or car window!

Now, Gopal ji was always treated to homemade sweets as a compulsory part of his daily worship. But once it so happened that, the bowl of milk meant for preparing his sweets, somehow slipped down from the hands of his Sanyasini mother. So, no milk was available anymore for preparing the sweets for Gopal ji. Nor could any milk be purchased, as all the shops were closed in that afternoon hour.

And the Sanyasini mothers did not want to disturb Sri Thakur. This was because, as per past precedent, he would inevitably instruct that a little milk, kept reserved for his own consumption, should be used to prepare sweets for his beloved Gopal ji instead! So, this option was ruled out as well.

Hence, the Sanyasini mothers began earnestly praying to Gopal ji for a solution that satisfies everybody. Suddenly it was discovered, to the utter joy of the worried Sanyasini mothers that, a cow and calf had arrived on their own - they were found to be patiently standing in the heat of afternoon sun near the closed main gate of the Ashram!

That milch cow was recognized to be the same one that was brought-in by the milkman to Ashram daily evening. Sanyasini mothers, overjoyed at this completely unexpected blessing, quickly arranged for the gate to be opened - the two animals then rushed in and the milch cow came to stand at that very spot where she used to wait during her daily milking hour. It was just astonishing!

Then the milkman, who was happily asleep at that hour in his home, was sent for. The amazed milkman came in reluctantly, thinking all the while, what was his milch cow doing at Ashram at that odd hour and wondering if she would give any milk in that afternoon heat! Again, a miracle happened: on that day, she yielded milk, that was far in excess of what she used to normally give on other days! And that quantity was more than sufficient for the preparation of sweets for dear Gopal ji! Divine magic was happening in front of the eyes of everyone!

Sri Thakur was delighted when this wonderful chain of events was related to him by equally happy Sanyasini mothers! He joyfully exclaimed, 'Look, it is our beloved Gopal ji Himself, who listened to your heartfelt prayers. It is his Divine Mercy that has made all these miracles possible!'

In such a manner, Gopal ji's Leela kept showering its Divine Grace at Ashram for a prolonged period. It is a truly glorious tale of Divine bliss!

"Puja needs to be performed - God has mandated it." - Sri Thakur

7.1.4 Daily Spiritual Discourse

Sri Thakur was like a giant spiritual magnet, whose unseen yet powerful aura used to attract so many devotees every day. This used to hold good for whichever Ashram Sri Thakur used to be stationed at any point of time: Baranagar, Suri or other Ashrams.

And then an event of tremendous goodness used to occur multiple times a day: Sri Thakur, the God Incarnate

Himself, used to read and explain the sacred words of God, contained in our holy Scriptures! Those sacred words, uttered by God Himself earlier and explained by God-Incarnate Himself (i.e., Sri Thakur) then, used to directly reach the ears of the fortunate devotees present...! Truly, how glorious this phenomenon was!

These Scriptures compulsorily included the holy trio of Srimad Bhagwat Gita, Sri Ramakrishna Kathamrita, and Upanishad. And as per the occasion, other holy books such as Sri Chaitanya Charitamrita, Sri Ramakrishna Mangal Kavya etc. were also read. And Sri Thakur had a unique method of conducting such discourses:

First, a portion of the concerned Scripture used to be read out and then, Sri Thakur used to explain that text in the light of Spirituality as well as science. Sri Thakur thus introduced the novel idea of explaining our ancient scriptures in terms of modern science! So, his discourses marked the wonderful blending of ancient Scriptural wisdom and modern Scientific knowledge!

And in a new twist, Sri Thakur used to often ask, at random, any devotee present as to what he had learnt that day. This custom had the salutary effect of keeping everyone alert during the entire duration of the discourse, as they knew beforehand that Sri Thakur could ask them questions at any moment.

Plus, as Sri Thakur used to emphasize so often, God is present within the heart of each one of us. So, a fresh perspective on the topic at hand used to emerge each and every time, a devotee used to answer the question posed by Sri Thakur!

As a result, the total atmosphere of those blissful discussions used to get enriched immeasurably! How wonderful the whole session used to be!

"Every day, all of you should take pains and ensure that 'Japa' should go on within your mind at all times amidst whatever you do." - Sri Thakur

7.1.5 'Sadhu Sammelan' (Conference of Monks)

Sri Thakur was a firm believer in the concept of unity in diversity of Hinduism. He gave this concept a unique name: United Nations organization, U.N.O of Religion. Basically, he wished that the followers of each particular path of Hinduism should adhere to their respective path and at the same time, respect other paths as well. That would bring in the much needed unity within Hinduism, the faith of the majority in India.

Towards the fulfilment of this noble mission, Sri Thakur used to periodically invite the respected Sanyasis and Sanyasini Mothers, representing different Ashrams of Hinduism. These respected religious figures used to gather together in a unique "Sadhu Sammelan" on the holy grounds of Sri Thakur's Ashram and then discuss some selected topic of Hinduism in the sacred presence of Sri Thakur himself. In this sequence, so many renowned Spiritual heads of different monasteries such as Sanyasini Durga Puri Maa, Sanyasini Gayatri Maa, Sri Mohanananda Brahmachari and others had come.

Sri Thakur used to repeatedly stress that it was the bounden duty of each individual, following any particular sect of Hinduism, to enhance the effectiveness of U.N.O of Hinduism. He was very clear in his mind that the cultivation of Spirituality in life by an individual is not meant for uplifting of only his own self. Rather Spirituality is meant for welfare of everyone. That is why he had given the clarion call for the formation of U.N.O of Hinduism.

And, in his invaluable opinion, the wonderful concept of 'global togetherness', as given in our holy Upanishad was the most appropriate philosophy for such U.N.O of Hinduism to come into practical existence.

"Through the habit of constant remembrance of God, we can create new channels of devotion to God in our brain. That is why Bhagavan Sri Krishna has laid so much stress upon 'Abhyas Yoga' in Gita."- Sri Thakur

7.1.6 "Mani Mandir" (Jewel Temple)

A long-cherished dream of Sri Thakur was realised with the inauguration of the temple of 'Mani Mandir' at Baranagar Ashram on 13th March 1967. Now, 'Mani Mandir' means the jewel temple - indeed this glass-walled temple used to shine like a sparkling jewel at night! And this beauty used to get enhanced even more by the reflection of that shining effulgence on the flowing waters of the holy river Ganga, on the bank of which Baranagar Ashram is located!

The principal Deity of this new temple was Maa Trinayani (a new form of Maa Kali), whose looks had flashed before Sri Thakur in the form of a 'Divine Vision'. And this appearance was quite different from the conventional appearance of Maa Kali. The holy name 'Trinayani' was given by Sri Thakur too.

Maa Trinayani is a four-armed Deity, blue in complexion, who holds a sword of lightning in one hand, while 'Kamandalu' (a pitcher of holy water) is there in Her second hand. Her other two hands shower blessings on devotees. And she stands on a beautiful lotus flower (instead of Lord Shiva) - altogether She has an unusual yet a beautifully Divine appeal.

Sri Thakur used to look upon Maa Trinayani just like his own daughter and was very fond of decorating Her with costly ornaments and new dresses everyday. Very interestingly, She used to tell Sri Thakur when Her decoration on any particular date was not up to Her liking. Then, as per Sri Thakur's instruction, new ornamentation had to be arranged for Her immediately. And, because She was considered to be maiden by Sri Thakur, red vermillion mark (an external symbol of married state) was never used for her adornment.

Then there also used to be joyful days, when Trinayani Maa used to be very happy with Her particular attire. Her delight used to get transmitted to Sri Thakur who then used to exclaim in bliss, "Just see! How radiantly beautiful does Maa look! She is truly glad today!" In this manner, a wonderful Leela used to go on between the God Incarnate Sri Thakur Satyananda and his beloved daughter, Trinayani Maa.

"We are all children of bliss - we have come to this Earth to stay on the path of bliss - at the end, we shall all go back to that eternal source of bliss." - Sri Thakur

7.1.7 Holy Name of God

The whole cosmos is vibration in its true essence and God is the Highest vibration, whose manifestation occurs in the form of Word. That is why, Word is God and God is Word. Hence, God and His sacred Name are one and the same. So, when we sincerely utter the Holy Name of God, then we are blessed by the Divine touch of God himself.

This is why all Incarnations of God in every single age have extolled the virtue of uttering the Holy Name of God at all times. In this modern age, Sri Thakur had also upheld the sanctity of the constant utterance of the Holy Name of God. He had always advised his devotees to take recourse to this all-powerful means for making steady progress on the Spiritual path.

"For getting complete fortification, it is important to pray to God, read sacred scriptures, cultivate noble thoughts, and always carry the Holy Image of God with oneself."- Sri Thakur

7.1.8 Tapasya

Spiritual austerity, 'Tapasya' was the hallmark of the sacred life of Sri Thakur and all his renunciate disciples (Sannyasi and Sanyasini Mothers) as well. The special features of this multi-faceted 'Tapasya' are highlighted here:

- Sri Thakur used to repeatedly emphasize that 'Tapasya', voluntary self-denial was the only means through which the dormant seed of Spirituality could be awakened within us and the gross desires of our physical body curbed.
- This is why Sri Thakur used to consider 'Tapasya' as desirable for all spiritual seekers in general and mandatory for spiritual renunciates in particular.
- On the day of Ekadashi (11th day of the lunar fortnight), Sri Thakur used to keep fast and observe complete silence for the whole day. The same example used to be followed by all his disciples as well - they used to spend the day in Japa and Dhyana in total silence.
- Inspired by Sri Thakur, his disciples would regularly carry out Japa and Dhyana in open courtyard of Ashram in the peak of summer heat in the afternoons and in the height of winter chill at nights.

- Similarly, those disciples used to often carry out 'Homa' during the entire night.
- Sometimes they used to sing 'Kirtan' throughout the night and even several nights together.
- And at other times, they used to stand on one foot and spend the whole night in carrying out Japa and Dhyana.
- These disciples also used to perform a novel form of Tapasya whereby they would go to a particular Temple, not by walking, but by nonstop rolling on the ground! This was called 'dandi' Tapasya - in this process, their bodies used to get badly scratched but they would remain completely indifferent to such bodily pain and would silently go on repeating the Holy Name of God till they reached their destination!

And Sri Thakur's blessing would always get showered on all his disciples, who would willingly subject themselves to these harsh spiritual austerities, through the sacred path of 'Tapasya'.

"In the Spiritual matter, the very first thought that comes to mind needs to be listened to and in the worldly affair, it is the second thought striking the mind that needs to be attended to."- Sri Thakur

7.2 Spreading Man-making Education

Swami Vivekananda had famously said, "Education is manifestation of perfection already in man". And Sri Thakur too was a firm believer in the astonishing power of such man-making education. That is why, he had opened an informal school for little children at Suri Ashram since its inception. Some unique features of this school were:

- First, this institution came into existence with only ten children on its roll.
- Second, the little children used to attend their classes out in the open, on a mattress spread on the ground, near a fruit tree in the Ashram compound. There was no furniture in the conventional sense of a school...!
- Second, the classes used to begin in a novel manner with 'Dhyana'. The little children used to meditate with eyes closed, while Sri Thakur used to stroll about in the class with a lighted stick of aromatic incense in his hand. And these obedient children used to open their eyes, only on hearing the signal of 'Sri Hari Ramakrishna', chanted by Sri Thakur. It was a unique practice indeed!
- The character of little children used to get enriched through daily moral instruction from Sri Thakur - he used to guide them on moulding their lives through the high ideals of constant devotion to God, their parents as well as their teachers.
- He also used to encourage these budding talents to have a high aim in life and start moving towards that aim right from their childhood.
- The powerful positive affirmation, "We shall grow up to be great" used to be daily chanted by him, for subsequent repetition by the little children. It was a very powerful auto-suggestion that used to profoundly impact their malleable minds.

In totality, 'Education' was held up by Sri Thakur as the best means of flowering of inborn talent of children and development of their character. For him, education was never meant to be degraded to a merely mechanical means of earning a living.

And Sri Thakur was a strong votary of education in the language of Sanskrit. He wanted to make learning of Sanskrit compulsory at all levels as this Divine language contains the key to formation of noble character through regular study of our holy scriptures written in Sanskrit.

Keeping all these ideals in view, the school of 'Sri Ramakrishna Vidyapeeth' was established by Sri Thakur at Suri in 1942. Gradually, schools came to be established at all other branch Ashrams as well. And for the purpose of imparting higher education, Sri Thakur laid the foundation of 'Sri Abhedananda Mahavidyalaya' at the town of Sainthia in Birbhum district.

Special Note:

Sri Thakur used to lay great emphasis on developing of unique talent of each child, granted to him by God, through the medium of education.

For example, if a child was found to be good in writing poems and stories, then Sri Thakur used to encourage him to excel in that direction. And if a child was found good to be in music, Sri Thakur used to encourage her to further refine that God given ability. In this manner, if a child was good in any domain of creativity, Sri Thakur used to encourage him or her all the way.

In this context, one of his most inspiring quotes is this: "The inner potential present within each individual is bound to flower to its full beauty provided that:

i. such potential should be exclusively meant for worship of God and
ii. such potential should get developed through virtuous means"

That's why Sri Thakur used to encourage his disciples to constantly pray: "Maa, please make us fulfil the specific Mission, to accomplish which, You chose to send us to this earth".

And finally mention must be made of the strong emphasis laid by Sri Thakur on "self-initiative" for learning any creative discipline. He used to firmly emphasise it was the only way in which originality of God- given talent could be preserved.

We have thus made an attempt, to highlight just the key points of Sri Thakur's wonderful philosophy of education and development, which would otherwise need scores of pages to describe at full length.

"Always remember God is keeping watch over you - He is guiding you - keep this ever in mind."- Sri Thakur

7.3 The Epitome of Compassionate Love

If we were ever to describe Sri Thakur in one word, then we can straightaway say he was the living personification of the virtue of "compassion".

As an instance of his innate generosity, during his college days, he used to give tuitions free of cost to a large number of poor students and provide them with books and monetary assistance, as and when required.

Even animals used to be recipients of his love and compassion. For example, one day he came across a sick and hungry stray dog while going to his college. His boundless empathy made him immediately get down from his bicycle and purchase some eatables from a nearby shop. Thereafter, with deep affection, he fed the starving animal with his own hand. Only then did he resume the journey to his college.

Many other incidents can be cited as well. All of them clearly revealed the inherently loving nature of Sri Thakur.

And inspired by him, his Sannyasi disciples also used to joyfully plunge into the noble arena of 'service to humanity' encompassing multiple forms such as providing food to the hungry during famine, distributing medicines to the afflicted throughout pandemics such as cholera, supplying medicines to the needy from the charitable Ashram dispensary and so on.

He used to always uphold the golden principle 'Serve God by serving humanity', as given by Bhagavan Sri Ramakrishna Dev, by exhorting his disciples: "Whenever you are providing a hungry person with food, then think that you are making food offering to God Himself. And similarly, when you are distributing among the needy, do so with the complete belief that God himself is standing in front of you. You are serving Him directly by helping such destitute people."

Here we can also share the exemplary way in which Sri Thakur used to arouse the inherent dignity of the so-called "untouchables", so cruelly treated in our society since long. In every village of Bengal and Bihar, where Ashrams were set up by Sri Thakur, he used to take special care to bring such marginalized people back into the main-fold of the society. And he always chose the Divine path of spirituality for carrying out this noble mission.

Sri Thakur used to re-ignite sense of self-respect among them by naming them 'Thakur Das' (servant of God) and assuring them that any occupation they pursue after uttering Holy name of God is a worthy one. In this context, we will be honoured to know that he had held a special ceremony in the Batikaar village of Birbhum district, wherein a large number of these so-called "low caste untouchables" had received the Grace of Sri Thakur, in front of holy sacrificial fire.

And after this ceremony, a few of them such as Chaitanya Dhangar had started leading such an admirably pure life that they became eligible to receive the highest blessings of 'Sanyas Diksha'!

Friends, it is truly uplifting to share with you these noble steps initiated by Sri Thakur in the cause of serving humanity at large.

"Infinite power lies within you - you can do everything - all obstacles are bound to prostrate themselves before you." - Sri Thakur

7.4 Bringing together Science and Spirituality

Sri Thakur was a genius in the truest sense of the word. One of the strongest indicators to support this statement would be his outstanding scientific temperament that was a part of his innate nature.

That's why, he was so fond of carrying out innovative experiments in science, right from his childhood. And later on, when he was firmly established in the path of Spirituality, then he used to love applying scientific concepts in this sacred arena also. How unique this was in the spiritual tradition of our country...!

For example, when devotees used to plead before Sri Thakur about their inability to achieve the requisite concentration during their daily 'Dhyana', he used to make them sit in front of multi-coloured bulbs and meditate. The colour of such bulb - white, light blue, green, yellow, red - used to be chosen by him as per the individual devotee's basic nature. In this manner he experimented with different colours and got good results in getting the desired level of concentration.

And, he used to love applying the concepts of various scientific disciplines such as physics, chemistry, biology, mathematics, psychology etc. to explain the abstract concepts of spirituality during his daily discourse. And he used to do it in such a manner that devotees with even non-science background could easily grasp his teachings. A few apt examples will serve to illustrate this point beautifully, though such instances are too numerous to be covered in this short account.

Let us take just one example: Sri Thakur used the concepts of Biology to explain the 5th shloka of the 10th chapter of the holy Gita during one of his daily discourses. To bring out the inner essence of this shloka, he took the help of the relevant chapter of Botany which says that the leaves of lotus plants, growing in water, contain pores covered by a cutaneous layer, on top of which there is another waxy layer. As a result, water can never wet those lotus leaves, even though they are always surrounded by water.

In the same manner, Sri Thakur said, this water can be considered to represent the gross material world filled with temptations, while the waxy layer can be thought as representing the protective covering of constant Devotion to God. So, a devotee remains untouched by the corrupting sins of this world due to the protective covering of the Grace of God.

Friends, there are numerous examples of such wonderful applications of science in Spirituality and you are referred to an admirable volume, "Vigyan-manaska Satyananda" ("Scientific-minded Satyananda"), penned by revered Swami Hirananda of Sri Satyananda Devayatan, for a comprehensive account of all such examples.

Suffice it to say that Sri Thakur magnificently combined the Eastern flavour of Spirituality and the Western flavour of science, in order to arrive at the total picture of Religion in its true sense.

"God is very merciful in this age - He will shower His grace upon you if you make even the slightest efforts." - Sri Thakur

7.5 Creating Divine literature

Sri Thakur was a vast Galaxy of knowledge with constant quest to learn all throughout his life. His genius of learning found its expression through multifarious channels: writing books, composing poems, framing song-lyrics, penning magazine-articles, scripting drama, music drama, dance drama...the list just goes on.

Equally exemplary was the way he used to constantly encourage his monastic disciples to take up the pen and bring-out their God-given talents by composing books, poems, songs etc. on their own. Thus, a rich treasury of Divine literature got built up in a short period, under the patronage of Sri Thakur.

Let us now have a bird's eye view of this magnificent treasury:

7.5.1 Monthly Ashram magazine "Bhabmukhey"

This is the signature publication of Sri Thakur's Ashram that comes out every month in Bengali till date. Its longevity is note-worthy indeed! And the unique name of this magazine, whose inaugural issue got published on the auspicious 'tithi' of 'Guru Purnima' on 17th July 1943, is derived from the Bengali word "Bhab mukhey", (meaning: staying in bliss) connoting the blessing uttered by Mother Goddess to Bhagavan Sri Ramakrishna Dev at the sacred temple of Dakshineshwar.

The initial issues of this monthly publication used to contain articles, stories, poems etc. on Religion, Spirituality, Philosophy and allied topics, penned by Sri Thakur, Sanyasi disciples, Sanyasini Mother disciples, as well as other writers also.

Now, this tradition is being continued by His successors at Ashram.

7.5.2 Books

Under Sri Thakur's Divine inspiration, a number of books began to be written, right from the inception of Suri Ashram. Examples of some initial publications of Ashram are: "Manjir" and "Bhajan Been". These publications contain collections of songs penned by Sri Thakur himself.

Sri Thakur always took a keen interest in the subject of Philosophy: he used to love brushing up his knowledge on the latest of this fascinating subject and teach it to his disciples at Ashram. Under his encouragement, his foremost disciple - Sanyasini Archana Maa - initially wrote a series of articles in the monthly Ashram magazine, covering the gist of the important theories of Philosophy. Later on, as per the instructions of Sri Thakur, all these articles in Bengali were compiled into one single volume and duly published under the beautiful name, 'Samanvayi Darshan' (Integrated Philosophy).

Afterwards, Sri Thakur himself wrote a comprehensive three-part book series entitled 'World Philosophy', containing salient points of all the major schools of thought in Eastern as well as Western Philosophy. Later on, continuing this learned trend, he also composed two more magnificent book-series entitled 'World Ethics' and 'World Psychology'. All of them stand for heights of erudition and are of the greatest help to the earnest seekers of knowledge.

Simultaneously, Sri Thakur continued to express his inner Divinity in form of poetry as well as prose. A writer - lyricist par excellence, he penned more than seven thousand songs, hundreds of poems, essays, articles and several books of great spiritual calibre. His books are especially notable for bringing out the topics of Divinity in a beautiful and aesthetic language. Currently, his collected works in English and Bengali are available in 8 Volumes.

Mention must also be made of the contributions by the monastic disciples of Sri Thakur to the collection of Divine literature of Ashram. Under his Divine guidance, Sanyasini Archana Maa wrote books like 'Sri Ramakrishna Mangal Kavya'- the poetical biography of Bhagavan Sri Ramakrishna Dev, 'Janani Saradeshwari' - biography of Holy Mother Sri Sarada Devi, 'Sri Ramakrishna Gita', thousands of songs, thousands of poems and so on.

Similarly, Sanyasini mother Sharana Maa wrote an account of the illustrious life of Swami Vivekananda. Another Sanyasini mother, Arati Maa composed a seven-volume book series, entitled 'Sharavana-Mangalam' (Listening to Divine Bliss), in a date-wise diary format, covering the daily life and teachings of Sri Thakur, over a long span of almost three decades. And there were more publications of other Sannyasi and Sanyasini mothers as well.

All in all, the Divine literature of Sri Thakur and his disciples continue to remain beacons of inspiration and joy for everyone aspiring to the follow the path of Spirituality.

"We need to be geared towards God in body, mind and speech." - Sri Thakur

7.6 Propagating Divine Culture

Sri Thakur was an embodiment of exquisitely refined taste in all aspects of his day-to-day living. This found its expression through his appreciation for our rich heritage of art and culture. That's why he always wanted to preserve and enrich it through spirituality.

He had an exceptionally broad outlook towards art and culture. To him, all its wide-ranging forms such as music, dance, theatre, painting, sculpture, embroidery and even cooking were independent avenues for getting connected to God. This was a truly unique facet of the Divine personality of Sri Thakur!

The following narrative tries to briefly touch upon his glorious contribution to the propagation of Divine art and culture all through his illustrious life:

7.6.1 Music

For Swami Vivekananda, music was the highest form of worship. In the same tradition, Sri Thakur considered music as one of the holy paths to reach God. He was a true devotee of music himself and that is why, so many artists of all-India repute used to love coming to Ashram and offering the homage of music at his lotus feet.

To fulfil this noble objective, a large number of renowned music artists came to him. They included Pandit Ravi Shankar, Pandit V G Jog, Pandit Omkarnath Thakur, Ustad Faiyaz Khan, Ustad Bade Ghulam Ali Khan, and so many others. Quite a few of them offered their musical tribute to Sri Thakur on more than one occasion.

Such devotion-soaked music, emanating straight from the heart of the artist, used to lead Sri Thakur to a deep state of meditation. And afterwards he used to bless them in a mood of joy, by saying, "The beautiful music, you have offered just now, has reached my ears during my meditation and I have tried to transmit its sacred vibrations to the Divine Presence of God. Know for sure such grace of God will greatly enhance the sweetness of your music".

Foreign musicians had also come to the holy presence of Sri Thakur quite a few times, as if pulled in by the magnetic aura of that Divine personality. One such notable figure was Pete Seeger, the acclaimed folk musician of USA. He had visited the Dubrajpur Ashram and delighted Sri Thakur and all others present on that day with American folk music. And at the end he had conclusively established that folk music of all countries have commonality in their nature especially, in their tunes.

One of the biggest qualities of Sri Thakur, already referred to earlier, was he knew how to encourage an individual artist and enable his potential to flower to its full glory. For example, Sri Rathin Ghosh was inspired by Sri Thakur to continuously polish his inborn talent of singing 'Kirtan' and subsequently Sri Ghosh went on to earn the title of 'Kirtan Kalanidhi'.

Another instance can be cited about the exemplary way in which Sri Thakur used to give boost to the folk music tradition of rural Bengal, especially its 'Baul' music tradition. He compiled lyrics of many such songs in folk dialect and catalysed the formation of a musician's group to promote this unique genre of music.

Most importantly, the musical genius of Sanyasini Archana Maa, the spiritual daughter of Sri Thakur, gradually bloomed to its full brilliance under the Divine guidance of her Guru and we have already made a mention of the thousands and thousands of songs composed by her.

And before concluding, we must make a mention of how the holy ritual of 'Arati' used to be carried out in a uniquely musical manner in Ashram temple. During this sacred ritual, a bouquet of devotional songs (composed by Sri Thakur, Sri Archana Maa and others) used to be offered as musical homage to God. In Ashram, 'Arati' used to be performed several times every day and the tribute of music was offered each time.

During 'Arati', some of the songs were sung in solo by Sri Thakur and Archana Maa, while the rest were sung in chorus by Sanyasini mothers. And the musical accompaniment on 'Tabla' used to be done by a Sanyasi disciple of Sri Thakur, while other musical instruments such as sitar, organ and harmonium were played by Sanyasini mothers.

Such songs of devotion to God used to surcharge the entire atmosphere of Ashram and that of its surroundings with subtle vibrations of wonderful Divinity. Everyone could distinctly experience this sacred phenomenon day after day.

In this beautiful manner, Sri Thakur Satyananda literally built up a musical treasure-chest of immense richness. These devotional songs, steeped in the eternal fragrance of Divinity, will forever remain an invaluable medium to connect all earnest spiritual seekers to God.

"The more you cultivate noble thoughts - the more you perform noble deeds - the more 'holy man' you will become - the more 'whole man' you will become." - Sri Thakur

7.6.2 Dramatics

Sri Thakur, true to his genius, had conceived the brilliant idea of utilizing non-conventional means such as theatre to spread the message of spirituality all around. That is why he composed and directed many plays, based on themes of Spirituality drawn from the Scriptures, sacred lives of God-Incarnates, holy lives of Saints, and other sources of Divinity. And he also motivated his monastic disciples such as Sri Archana Maa, Swami Nirvedananda ji and others, to compose scripts of plays in the same manner.

Some of the noted plays were: 'Tulsi Das', 'Naam Dev', 'Madhusudan Dada' etc. These plays used to be enacted regularly at Suri and other Ashrams, as part of festive calendar and on other occasions as well.

These plays had several distinguishing features. First and foremost, these were based on devotion to God. Second, they were often used to be enacted on the spur of the moment, without any kind of rehearsal whatsoever. Third, often little children used to be the main actors in such plays.

For example, under instructions of Sri Thakur, plays used to be often enacted extempore on open grounds. Here small children used to act, sing as well as dance. And each of them used to be given full freedom by Sri Thakur to make the use of his inborn talent to compose all the dialogues then and there and enact the best he could.

This used to be Sri Thakur's tried and tested method for arousing the creative potential, granted by God, to each child, so that he can make continual progress in achieving the God-given Mission of his life. This was a wonderful prescription for the flowering of innate Divinity of a child.

And the marvellous way small children as well as the monastic disciples of Sri Thakur used to act in these plays used to attract applause from everyone. The audience used to wonder how such amateur actors can play their individual roles so brilliantly. And it is a fact that the standard of acting by these amateur actors in some of these plays used to be so high that, in the opinion of learned people, such levels of excellence could be favourably compared to the best of professional actors on the theatre stages of Kolkata!

And, last but not the least, we need to make note of the fact that Sanskrit drama also used to be staged at Baranagar Ashram - this truly shared showed the love and respect of Sri Thakur towards the Divine language of Sanskrit.

In this manner, the seeds of spirituality and religion used to get spread through the novel medium of devotion-soaked plays of Ashram.

"Always repeat the Holy Name of God." - Sri Thakur

7.6.3 Dance

Divine culture expresses itself through various avenues such as music, theatre, painting, sculpture, and so on. In this sequence, dance was another creative medium, wonderfully utilized by Sri Thakur for strengthening the roots of devotion to God.

For this noble mission, informal sessions used to be regularly held in Ashram compound, where small children (with no previous training) used to present extempore recitals of dance in sync with devotional music. And, these little dancers used to even present different 'mudra' (specific steps of dance), composed on the spot! Initially feeling shy, the children used to start dancing freely later on! All this wonder used to be made possible through the Grace of Sri Thakur!

And Sri Thakur also composed several dance-dramas, whose main theme was devotion to God. The first such dance-drama, written in Bengali, was "Borsha Baran" (Welcoming Monsoon) - Sri Thakur got it enacted by the children of devotees along with the students of a local School. And as per his custom, he did not engage any expert to train the children how to dance and made them learn on their own under the informal guidance of their elders.

For dance recitals on special occasions (such as festive programs), he used to entrust Sanyasini mother Sharana Maa with the responsibility of guiding the dances of the participating children during rehearsals. And she used to fulfil that responsibility with total sincerity.

At times, during such rehearsals, Sri Thakur himself used to suggest improvement in the dancing steps of the participants. He could do so easily because of his inborn sense of artistic refinement. And, when such devotion-soaked dance recitals used to be finally presented on stage, the audience used to get moved by the strong vibrations of Spirituality!

In this manner, the artistic medium of dance was uniquely employed by Sri Thakur to encourage talent development among children, on one hand and spread the message of Spirituality among the masses, on the other hand.

"Ensure that you always keep repeating Holy Name of God within your mind." - Sri Thakur

7.6.4 'Sudhi Sammelan'(Conference of Scholars)

Sri Thakur is a role model to all of us because of his quest to learn all through his Divine life. This quest used to be evident in his love for interacting with scholars in various disciplines of learning - these experts used to keep on coming to the Ashram, pulled in by the magnetic aura of the God-Incarnate. They included both Indians as well as foreign scholars. While their informal meetings with Sri Thakur used to take place throughout the year, conferences of scholars used to be especially arranged at the time of important festivals at Ashrams.

Now, let us look at some of the interesting tit bits of these events:

Conference of Indian scholars

In annual 'Sudhi Sammelan' held at Ashram, scholars - poets, authors, philosophers, professors and many other learned people used to be regularly invited. Sri Kumud Ranjan Mallick, Sri Naren Deb etc. were notable figures from the domain of Literature, while Dr Satish Chattopadhyay, Dr Mahendra Nath Sarkar etc. were some of the stalwart Philosophers. Mention must also be made of the renowned historian, Dr R C Majumdar who came over several times.

Sri Thakur, with abiding faith in our rich heritage of Sanskrit language, also used to love to meet Sanskrit scholars such as Dr Gouri Nath Shastry, Dr Rama Chowdhury and others, who used to regularly come to Ashram, attracted by the wonderful aura of Sri Thakur.

To illustrate the high quality of discussions at these scholar's conferences, we can refer to an actual session that occurred as a part of celebration of birth anniversary of Holy Mother, Maa Sarada in 1955. In that session, an eminent scholar had given a wonderful analogy to bring out the difference between Sri Ramakrishna Dev and Maa Sarada, in respect of granting the sacred 'Mantra Diksha' to their devotees.

This learned scholar had pointed out that Sri Ramakrishna Dev resembled Professor Shambhu Bandopadhyay, a very strict professor who did not allow any student to pass the exam unless he had worked really hard to perform well in that paper.

On the other hand, Maa Sarada was like Professor Ashu Mukhopadyay, a very lenient examiner, who used to allow a large number of students to easily pass the exam, irrespective of the level of their individual performance in that paper.

This was a very apt analogy as Sri Ramakrishna Dev was extremely choosy in the matter of selection of his disciples and granting them the holy spiritual initiation; on the other hand, Maa Sarada was very liberal in granting it to anyone approaching Her.

On hearing such a beautiful comparison, the whole audience had erupted with joy. And Sri Thakur, seated on the wings of the stage, had also appreciated such high-quality thinking.

In this manner, under Sri Thakur's patronage, these annual conferences of scholars used to add immense value to diversity of thoughts in spirituality and religion.

Meeting with Foreign scholars

Foreign scholars used to regularly visit Sri Thakur's Ashram on various occasions. Examples included American Professors - Dr Smith and Dr James Whitehurst, French philosophers - Sylvain levy, Japanese Professor - J G Oshara and several other scholarly figures.

In fact, Dr Smith, after meeting Sri Thakur at Suri Ashram, stayed on for nearly one month there. And during this period, he used to enthusiastically participate in the holy rituals of Ashram such as Homa, Arati etc., in compliance with the valuable advice of Sri Thakur, "Look Smith, you will have to know about the spirituality of India in order to understand the pulse of India and to understand the spirituality of India, you will have to voluntarily adopt a life of hardships." That is why he used to love accompanying Sri Thakur in going to 'Raas Ban', an Ashram located in between the banks of two rivers. And there, he used to merrily spend nights lying on an improvised bed made-up of hay...!

We can also mention about two sons of USA, Levy and Cruise, who wanted to learn about the true essence of Indian philosophy. That is why they chose to come to Suri Ashram and directly learn from Sri Thakur about the intricacies of different schools of thought in Indian philosophy. In this manner, they also opted for a life of austerity in order to quench their thirst for knowledge. And deeply enriched with their learning at the lotus feet of Sri Thakur, they went back to their parent country happily.

"To be virtuous requires strong will to be good, as its foundation." - Sri Thakur

7.6.5 'Shishu Sammelan' (Get-together of Children)

Sri Thakur's earnest effort was to spread Divinity among all strata of the population. That is why the children, the future of our country, were always included among the audience of his spiritual endeavours.

In this sequence, a unique cultural event called 'Shishu Sammelan' used to be regularly organized at Ashram as a part of the annual festive calendar. In these events, only the children could take part either as participants or as audience as well. Here, the child-artists used to present a wonderful bouquet of cultural programs comprising of recitation, singing, dancing and other items to the children's audience.

And as a novel gesture, the Chairman of these events used to be a child always! This unique practice used to be followed, even when renowned writers of children's fiction such as Mr Bimal Ghosh, Mr Prabhat K Basu etc. used to grace these programs, as the Chief Guest on special invitation.

Truly, the way these conferences were organized, used to be unique in all respects! Such events used to go a long way towards the spread of Divine culture among the tiny tots, the citizens of our country tomorrow.

"God dwells in each of our hearts. Go on praying to Him. He will cause your mind to get focused towards Divinity." - Sri Thakur

7.7 Outlook towards Earning Livelihood

Sri Thakur always upheld the principle of "work as worship". That's why he used to encourage his renunciate disciples (the Sanyasis and the Sanyasini mothers) to acquire higher educational qualifications and then, serve as Teachers in the schools run under the aegis of his Ashrams.

Encouraged by him, quite a few of them went on to earn BA, MA and even Ph.D. degrees and then, serve as Teachers in Schools and Colleges set up by Sri Thakur. As he used to rightly emphasise, they could earn their living independently that way and thus, avoid depending on anyone for meeting their needs.

And He used to always encourage his householder disciples to work sincerely in their chosen vocations such as service, business etc. and earn their livelihood by honest means. He was fully sympathetic towards them as he knew they were carrying huge financial burden on their shoulders in this age of relentless price-rise and competition. But at the same time, he also used to emphasise to them about the need to cultivate the virtue of contentment and joyfully accept whatever one earns, as the Blessings of God.

In the same vein, He always used to motivate the students of his schools to study hard, acquire high qualifications and get good jobs in order to earn well and take care of their parents, on one hand and contribute to the economic welfare of the country, the other hand.

And last but not the least, he always used to inspire everyone to contribute a part of his earnings towards charity for the upkeep of Religious Institutions such as Ashrams and Temples. That's because, as He rightly used to stress, everything we earn in this life is only because of the Grace of God.

This, in a nutshell, is the gist of Sri Thakur's outlook on the economic necessity of earning a livelihood.

"The hallmark of Divinity is a disciplined life." - Sri Thakur

Comment of Surrender

Friends, as repeatedly stated throughout this account, we can only marvel at the infinite expanse of the Divinity of Sri Thakur Satyananda. Even numerous volumes would not suffice to do proper justice to this ocean. So, I would like to surrender to Sri Thakur and beg His permission to stop my pen here. The substantive part of this narrative ends here.

And I earnestly pray to Sri Thakur to enable this author to document more details in companion volumes of this book and make those volumes see the light of the day in the shortest possible time.

"Whenever you pick up anything for study, then read it with wholehearted concentration - don't take up anything else - remember, a rolling stone gathers no moss." - Sri Thakur

CHAPTER EIGHT

Unique Contributions of Sri Thakur

Sri Thakur Satyananda was a Divine genius, who left his indelible mark, on each area of life touched by him. These encompass a very broad range of domains such as religion, spirituality, art, culture, education, training, philanthropy, social reforms, economic livelihood, and so on.

While we have already seen his unique contributions, in each of these areas, here is a recap for our easy reference:

i. Puja:

It is often said that Sarada Devi (consort of Bhagavan Sri Ramakrishna Dev) is the Mother Goddess Herself. But to demonstrate this in-ground reality is in a completely different league altogether. And Sri Thakur Satyananda did so, through the unique ceremony of 'Sarada-Durga Puja', held annually at his Baranagar Ashram. Even at the time of writing this account, this is probably the only place, where Sarada Devi is literally worshipped as Goddess Durga.

i. Ashram:

A mighty oak lies hidden in a tiny acorn. In the same manner, the Suri Ashram, which started in a small manner with just a handful of devotees in 1939, gave rise to branch Ashrams at so many locations in Bengal as well as Bihar, within quite a short period of time.

iii. Leela of Sri Gopal ji:

Sri Thakur was the Incarnation of Bhagavan Sri Narayan, one of whose forms is Gopal ji. Hence, the unique Leela of Sri Gopal ji was, in effect, the unique Leela of Sri Thakur Himself.

iv. Daily Spiritual Discourse:

The way Sri Thakur used to unify spirituality as well as science, in his daily discourse at the Ashram, is truly unparalleled in the chronicles of spiritual tradition in India!

v. United Nations Organization of Religion:

This was another novel contribution of Sri Thakur in conceptual form. If this idea actually gets implemented in its true spirit, then it will bring in the much-desired unity among different sects of Hinduism.

vi. Education:

Sri Thakur always emphasized that, the God-given talent of a child can flower to its fullest potential, if virtuous means are adopted during that unfolding process and if worship of God is its ultimate aim. This was one of his note-worthy contributions in the domain of education and development.

vii. Compassion and Love:

In this arena, Sri Thakur's unique contribution lay in the complete uplifting of the so-called 'low-caste untouchable' through granting of sacred 'Sanyas Diksha' to the spiritually deserving individuals among them.

viii. Divine Art and Culture:

In this domain, the unique contribution of Sri Thakur lay in the use of non-conventional means like theatre for spreading the spiritual vibrations among the masses.

ix. Shishu Sammelan:

This was a truly astonishing contribution of Sri Thakur in arousing the latent potential for excellence, granted by God, to each child. That's why he conceived of the unique idea of having a small child be the Chairman of these conferences, where literary figures (as reputed as Sri Prabhat Kiran Basu and others) used to be invited to be the Chief Guest.

x. Adoption of Monastic life by Entire Families:

Finally, we would like to make a special mention of Sri Thakur's absolutely novel contribution: the adoption of monastic life by entire families under his Divine inspiration!

Here, let me try to paint a picture of what usually happens when an individual decides to adopt a life of

Spirituality: - he gradually awakens to the futility of material life and starts developing an urge towards renunciation, as the dormant seed of spirituality sprouts within him. As a result, he decides to leave his household and go to a suitable Guru. And after carrying out austerities under Guru's guidance for a prolonged period of time, he gradually makes spiritual progress, which enables him to get blessed with the sacred vows of 'Brahmacharya' and later on, 'Sanyas' in due course of time.

But his other family members remain unaffected: initially they try to actively dissuade him from the path of spirituality and failing that, they continue their worldly life as usual. They remain sceptical about Spirituality and at times, they even display open hostility towards it.

Under the Divine influence of Sri Thakur, however, something radically different began to occur! And this was the unprecedented event of whole families taking shelter under Sri Thakur and then adopting the life of renunciation!

Normally, one member of a family, after meeting Sri Thakur at his Ashram, used to feel deeply attracted to the life of spirituality, and then, later on, join the Ashram fraternity. But soon the magnetic attraction of Sri Thakur used to cast its irreversible spell over the rest of the family as well. And lo and behold! The new Monk's father, mother, siblings - everyone used to gladly surrender themselves at the lotus feet of Sri Thakur and become monks too!

There are so many examples to illustrate this unparalleled magic of Sri Thakur. Just as an example, we can quote the name of Sri Satinath, a middle-class householder, who initially adopted the life of celibacy under Sri Thakur's encouragement, and in due course, the rest of his family of wife and three sons adopted the monastic life as well.

We can also cite the example of three sisters of the town of Suri joining Sri Thakur's Ashram and receiving vows of 'Brahmacharya' and later on, 'Sanyas'. They were the Sanyasini Mothers: Sharana Maa, Arati Maa and Aradhana Maa.

And the most appropriate examples would be that of the adoption of spiritual life by respected Sanyasini Archana Maa and her father in pre monastic life, Swami Nirvedananda ji - both of whom were counted among the foremost disciples of Sri Thakur.

The above examples are just samples and serve to illustrate the magnificent spiritual aura of Sri Thakur.

"Always keep your mind attuned towards the Higher Plane - be it in the spiritual matter or be it in the worldly affair." - Sri Thakur

CHAPTER NINE

Relevance of Sri Thakur in 21st Century

Friends, now that we are on the verge of reaching the end of this account of homage to Sri Thakur, what have we really learned? What are our takeaways? And most importantly, how can we apply our learning in our day-to-day life?

All the above questions become supremely relevant, as each one of us continues to grapple with life in the 21st century, where daily challenges have increased beyond imagination. Just one example of this complexity is the advent of the ubiquitous smartphone. So let me try to answer these vital questions by begging the Grace of Sri Thakur, whose very life was his teaching: -

First and foremost, Sri Thakur used to lay the highest stress on constantly repeating holy name of God. In fact, his golden advice was to repeat the Holy Name of God with every single in-breath and every single out-breath.

So dear friends, let each one of us adopt this honourable way of living - this easy path of remembrance of God can help us remain connected with God 24/7 in our life. It's quite possible that many times we'll falter as we start this new habit - many times, we'll forget to repeat the Holy Name of God - many times, we'll go back to our old sensuous way of living.

But all these do not matter in the least. The moment we remember that we have stopped repeating the Holy Name of God, that very moment we can resume. Trust me, this one single effort is going to bring in the most magical transformation in our life!

Second, Sri Thakur used to lay the greatest stress on the companionship of Holy Men and cultivating the virtue of moral purity in day-to-day life. Friends, right now all of us possess a smartphone - in fact, many of us own more than one smartphone. This powerful device, however, is a double-edged sword, which can be used both ways: good as well as bad.

Hence, let us beg the grace of Sri Thakur so that we develop the strength of character to always use the smartphone in a virtuous manner. Let us start by exercising our God-given 'power of choice' by opting to use our smartphones to daily visit the websites of sacred Religious and Spiritual Institutions.

And when we pursue the path of Spirituality through this modern means, then blessings of God are bound to get showered on our life - this is because God is good and good is God and so consciously choosing the path of goodness leads us to God.

Most importantly, Sri Thakur has done a yeomen service to humanity at large by abolishing all the conventional differences between the spiritual life and the so-called secular life. This implies that besides the accepted path of worshipping God such as Puja, Japa, Dhyana, Reading Scriptures, etc., even the mundane activities of our day-to-day life such as Work qualify to be one of the acceptable means of revering God! So let us worship God by any means that suits our lifestyle - our lives will get blessed many times over.

"Keep on persevering towards your goal with strong faith." - Sri Thakur

CHAPTER TEN

A Humble Submission

Friends, with the grace of Sri Thakur Satyananda, a modest attempt has been made to offer homage to him by painting this short sketch of his illustrious life in words. This is just like the way we pay our homage to Mother Ganga, through offering Her own waters to Herself.

However, as already stated at the very beginning of this volume, full justice can hardly be done to the Infinite expanse of his Godly life in such a brief account. So, all that has been attempted is, just touch upon the salient points only.

After going through this humble narrative, if even one reader is inspired to know more about the sacred life of Sri Thakur, I'll consider my modest effort to have partially met its aim. He can do so by visiting the comprehensive website: *sreesatyanandamahapeeth.com.* And he is also welcome to visit any of the Ashrams of Sri Thakur. The addresses of the main Ashrams in Kolkata are:

i) Sri Ramakrishna Ashram,
1, Pran Krishna Saha Lane, Baranagar,
Kolkata - 700036

ii)Sree Satyananda Devayatan
1, Ibrahimpur Road, Jadavpur,
Kolkata - 700032

It is well said that an ounce of practice is worth a thousand words. Hence, the ultimate test of the effectiveness of reading an account of homage to Sri Thakur will be to what extent we are getting inspired to mould our own life as per the golden standards of His Saintly life. That is why, as we go through this account, it is imperative that we simultaneously reflect on our own life so that we gain the right direction for our life as well.

Thereafter, through earnest prayers to Sri Thakur, we can start bringing in positive changes in our lives in a gradual manner. How much we are thus able to actually elevate ourselves is less important. What truly matters is that we begin to move in the righteous direction.

And this is because, as aptly uttered by Bhagavan Ramakrishna Dev, as we start moving towards the Holy town of Kashi (representing virtues), the worldly town of Kolkata (the stronghold of vice) will automatically start receding further and further away from us.

With these words, I hereby place my modest offering at the lotus feet of Sri Thakur Satyananda and pray for his compassionate love and Grace in our lives.

“Keep moving forward by keeping faith on one particular path.”- Sri Thakur

“Jai Maa”

CHAPTER ELEVEN

The Transition to The Sacred Path of 'Monkhood'

All Incarnates carry the seed of Godliness within them since their birth - at the appropriate time, this seed sprouts and starts giving rise to a gigantic tree of Spirituality, that would give shade and comfort to the entire humanity one day. And as we'll see in this Chapter, this eternal principle was very much true for Sri Thakur also.

Satyabrata, in due course of time, finished his schooling and got enrolled in college to pursue higher education. Right from this point of time onward, he made up his mind to opt for the sacred path of 'Sanyas' and eschew the trifling pleasures of worldly life. The inner urge for this path, ever-present since his childhood, got transformed into a firm resolve at the starting point of his college.

So, on one hand, he regularly attended college; on the other hand, he continued his 'Sadhana' at the same pace at home. And now the sacred books of scriptures began to accompany him always: studying them frequently became his habit.

The noble path of spirituality thus came to co-exist with academics in his daily routine - during the day, he used to studiously attend his classes at college and on coming back home, he used to go back to his 'Sadhana'. Now, I shall relate a thrilling incident to illustrate the astounding level of his concentration during this 'Sadhana'!

One day, he was sitting in his room, completely absorbed in 'Dhyana'. And after a while, his younger sister happened to come in with a bowl of milk for him. However, she got the shock of her life to discover that, a huge cobra was already present in that room and the deadly serpent had spread its massive hood over her brother's head! The bowl slipped from her terrified hand and her frightened cries for help alerted the rest of the household, who rushed to Satyabrata's room! Fortunately, this frightening spectacle came to end after a while, as the cobra lowered its hood on its own and disappeared quietly.

The whole scenario represented nothing short of Divine symbolism: it clearly indicated to everyone that Satyabrata was Lord Shiva Himself - that's why the cobra, His ever-faithful companion had appeared, in order to pay its respect to the Lord Supreme! And, many such unusual events continued to occur, all of which pointed out to Satyabrata's Divine nature. In this manner, his Godly nature started gradually unfolding before his entire family!

In due course of time, Satyabrata completed his Intermediate, Bachelor's and Master's degree from the University of Calcutta. During this period, as his 'Sadhana' kept on increasing in intensity, it did not escape the attention of his alarmed family, who got worried that he would become a monk in the future and leave them forever. Therefore, his well-off family started trying their best to bring him back to the lures of the material world, through the temptation of marriage. Satyabrata, however, firmly refused despite facing repeated scolding from his father.

And at times, such family pressure used to get so intense, that once he even tried to end his life by trying to jump off the terrace of his house. Luckily, in the nick of time, his youngest brother managed to grab hold of him from the back and thus, save his life. Ultimately, Satyabrata's steadfast resolve to remain celibate, made his family capitulate. And thereafter, no further pressure was brought upon him for entering into marital bondage.

In this context, we recall how Bhagavan Buddha Dev grew up amidst the abundance of a kingdom and yet chose to renounce all such material riches in favour of the noble path of 'Sanyas'. The same trend was now visible in the life of Bhagavan Satyananda Dev also.

In this manner, each and every stage in the life of a God-Incarnate serves as a role model. That is why the study of their sacred lives is so valuable for us.

"The main thing is to surrender to God. He always protects the one who surrenders to him." - Sri Thakur the temptation of marriage. Satyabrata, however, firmly refused despite facing repeated scolding from his father.

And at times, such family pressure used to get so intense that once he even tried to end his life by trying to jump off the terrace of his house. Luckily, in the nick of time, his youngest brother managed to grab hold of him from the back and thus save his life. Ultimately Satyabrata's steadfast resolve to remain celibate, made his family accept it, and there was no further pressure on him [illegible]

[illegible] so valuable.

"The main thing is to [illegible]

Prayers

- Maa, we are offering our humble homage at your Lotus feet!
- Only due to Your Infinite Grace, this humble account could be written!
- Please have mercy and forgive all the mistakes made here.
- And, we pray that may this account help us in finding the righteous direction for our lives.

"Jai Maa"

9 798886 672916

Printed by Libri Plureos GmbH in Hamburg,
Germany